HAUS CURIOSITIES

Integrity in Public Life

About the Contributors

Claire Foster-Gilbert is the founder director of the Westminster Abbey Institute. A public philosopher and author, Foster-Gilbert has played an instrumental role in the medical research ethics field and has led efforts to shift the Church's thinking on environmental issues.

Vernon White was Canon Theologian of Westminster Abbey from June 2011 until October 2018 and is a Visiting Professor at King's College London. Canon White was a member of the steering group for the Westminster Abbey Institute since its inception in 2013 and, from 2016, also served as Sub-Dean.

Jane Sinclair is Rector of St Margaret's Church, Westminster Abbey and chair of Westminster Abbey Institute. She was installed as a Canon of Westminster in September 2014. Previously, she was Archdeacon of Stow and Lindsey (Diocese of Lincoln) and has worked in parish and cathedral ministry and in theological education.

Edited and with an Introduction by Claire Foster-Gilbert

INTEGRITY IN PUBLIC LIFE

Vernon White, Claire Foster-Gilbert, and Jane Sinclair

First published by Haus Publishing in 2019
4 Cinnamon Row
London SW11 3TW
www.hauspublishing.com

The right of the authors to be identified as the authors
of this work has been asserted in accordance with
the Copyright, Designs and Patents Act 1988

A CIP catalogue record for this book is
available from the British Library

Print ISBN: 978-1-912208-70-8
Ebook ISBN: 978-1-912208-71-5

Typeset in Garamond by MacGuru Ltd

Printed in Czech Republic

Every effort has been made to trace the copyright holders and obtain
permission to reproduce the material quoted in this book. The
publisher would be pleased to rectify any omissions in subsequent
printings of the book should they be drawn to our attention.

Contents

Acknowledgements

Sincere thanks are due to the Dean and Chapter of Westminster, the Council of Reference, Fellows and Steering Group of Westminster Abbey Institute, Frances D'Souza, Ruth Cairns, Harry Hall, Alice Horne, Kathleen James, Seán Moore, Clare Moriarty, Barbara Schwepcke and Jack Straw.

Introduction

Claire Foster-Gilbert

Is integrity a necessary quality in a leader? The rise of populism across the world has introduced some doubt. Perhaps successful leadership is born not of integrity and moral courage, not of universalist principles that recognise the dignity of all humans, not of a strong intention to serve the needs of the poorest and most vulnerable, and not of a commitment to restoring the ecological health of the planet, but rather of a clear, single-minded focus on promoting the interests of your people and ignoring the needs of everyone and everything else, even actively denying them if they are obstacles to the flourishing of your own kind. After all, such a clear focus does produce results – of a kind.

Westminster Abbey Institute resists this doubt, not least because Westminster Abbey herself came into being within a tradition, Christianity, that has defined leadership as the role of a vulnerable and wounded healer whose love leads to ultimate sacrifice for the sake of all. Out of that same tradition a world view emerges – more often seen in the breach than otherwise, I fear – that cannot perceive anyone or anything as expendable. There is no place called 'away' where we can throw things. There is no person called 'other' whom we can deny or destroy if they stand in our way. As there is no 'other' to fight,

Christian leadership has to find a way of expressing itself that holds 'the all' – everyone and every issue – in its awareness, even if our responsibility is only for some part of the whole. This world view is of a unified, interdependent cosmos, every part of which affects every other part. The cosmos itself, in other words, has integrity: it is held together thanks to this interaction of its parts. Ignoring this fact or denying it only masks future harm. We can be on the first-class deck of the ship of the universe quaffing champagne and living in luxury paid for by the destruction of other humans' dignity and the health of the natural world, but the ship will sink if we continue to live in such a way, and we will all go down with it.

The premise of this book, then, is that integrity needs to be manifest in public life and service, however difficult and demanding that may be. These essays, edited versions of Westminster Abbey Institute lectures from 2017, explore the meaning of integrity for the individual public servant, for public service institutions, and for the public whom these servants seek to serve.

In his essay 'Integrity and the Individual: Keeping Conscience Alive', Vernon White offers three interlinked characteristics – sincerity, principles, and 'moral irony' – each of which is necessary to guarantee integrity but none of which is sufficient alone. Integrity could not exist without the first of these, sincerity, but a politician, for example, who is entirely sincere in their attempts to lead aright and uses only this criterion as a guide, may easily be led astray. It is not enough to believe sincerely. Sincerity on its own does not exonerate a leader whose decisions, made on that basis, turn out to have dire consequences; 'I meant well' is a lame excuse for destroying lives and can be surprisingly self-centred. Principles, argues White, should also be present in a leader of integrity: principles that have been tried and tested over time, agreed by others, and that are believed to be in the best interests of those you serve. These are not self-centred, but principles alone are not enough either. An idealistic and rigid adherence to principles can fail to serve just as much as self-centred best intentions can: every situation is different and requires its own response, so principles should guide this response, but they should not determine it. Unlike Kant, who believed that one must never lie (even if it puts another in danger) because it failed his categorical imperative,[1] we must recognise the need for flexibility in the application of our principles – otherwise these, too, become self-centred, even fanatical, as we attend to our own moral adherence and disregard the wellbeing of others in so doing. The third necessary characteristic of integrity that White explores is 'moral irony', a term he coins to address the need to hold together sincerity, principles, *and* the reality of the context in which one's leadership is being exercised. Holding these together is hard, White acknowledges. The ability to do so, which we recognise in others when they have it, develops over time through exposure to traditions and stories that show us what sort of life emerges from integrity and that teach deep honesty and sound principles, principles that can then become natural for us.

My essay on integrity in institutions explores the ways in which establishments have suppressed or undermined individual integrity, but it argues that without the stabilising effect of institutions, we are lost in a sea of choice – our increasingly anxious, precarious selves finding that they are unable to lead or even live well. For example, politicians often start their careers wanting to change the world but are slowly ground down by the sheer effort, complexity, and amount of compromise that absolutely any change requires in order to be enacted in law. And yet the process of enacting laws, cumbersome as it may seem, guards against ideas being rushed into legislation and later turning out to be flawed. The Civil Service 'sausage machine' that turns politicians' ideas into policy can, in so doing, turn the public – whom the ideas were meant to serve – into mere statistics and the civil servants creating and delivering them into mere automata. And yet policies need to be thought through dispassionately and impartially. The Royal Academy can destroy the inspiration of artists by trying to define art when, by its nature, art should burst any bounds. And yet without the Royal Academy, art would not be taught and it would not be seen. The Royal Society defines and limits scientific endeavour, but also promotes and furthers it. I argue that institutions, which have such an important stabilising role as custodians of values and practices, must themselves continually rediscover their own integrity. They must do this precisely through the responsible agency of the individuals working in them. Institutions and individuals are integral to one another.

Jane Sinclair's essay on the public we serve uses the town of Rotherham, where she was parish priest for many years, as an exemplar of the public, it having been identified as the place that most closely resembles the overall demographic of the country as a whole.[2] Public policymaking that meets the needs of people is a difficult, high art. Our individual experience of the consequences of policies is how we meet and know policy, not the clever and complex analysis of matrices of identified needs in different population types. But policies also drive the kind of society that we are. Sinclair asks 'How can our democratic processes better inform, reflect, and enable the creation of a good, generous, and caring society, one that seeks to curb our human tendency to cause harm to others and promotes instead the common good?' She proposes policies that drive or promote trust and do not undermine it. Integrity – that is to say, making yourself worthy of trust by means of consistency, honesty, and transparency – is necessary, but so is hope: hope that the project of making a democratic society work for the good of all is worth the effort because it will in some way succeed. If Rotherham has found its way to such a place, and Sinclair shows how it has, then we should all harbour such integrity and hope.

Is the current rise of narrow self-interest and bellicose posturing a last-ditch shout of greed and fear, the *reductio ad absurdum* of late-twentieth-century individualism and self-expression? After all, individualism was, in its day, a well-intended and idealistic reaction against the conformist group mentality that had given so much destructive power to fascism, communism, and stultifying social norms. As the global threat of ecological harm rises in the international consciousness, we are seeing a tardy but inexorable move away from independence and towards interdependence and collaboration with one another and with the planet. The angry reaction is, we might hope, short lived. But it may be that, like Rotherham, we have to pass through a time of reckoning if we are to live and breathe, not just think and talk about, our interdependent moral purpose, our need for one another – in short, our global integrity – again.

If we are hoping to rediscover integrity in our twenty-first-century world, these three essays should help. They are predicated on the belief that integrity is critical to leadership in public service, whether in individuals, institutions, or communities. And in exploring what integrity means in these different contexts, they also demonstrate how valuable it is for the art and craft of government, at every level.

Integrity and the Individual:
Keeping Conscience Alive

Vernon White

Addressing an American audience on the importance of integrity in public life a few years ago, a distinguished lawyer described the reaction.[3] The audience broke into instant applause just at the title of the lecture. Simply the word 'integrity' triggered a reaction. Like the sight of water in a desert, it was perceived to be something infinitely valuable, vital, scarce – and all too often, only a mirage.

I suspect many UK audiences would feel the same way. We would agree that integrity is critically important; that it is a foundational virtue; that it is rightly one of the seven great principles of public life set out by the Nolan committee;[4] that it is a vital disposition for any public servant of any political stance; and that it is a prerequisite of the trust so crucial for public life to function. We would also probably agree that it is widely perceived to be scarce; that a perceived *lack* of integrity – corruption, dishonesty, hypocrisy – is at the heart of a current pathology of distrust and cynicism felt about public life. But what I am less sure we know or agree about is what this elusive but desirable 'integrity' really is. It is a totemic word, but where does it come from and what does it mean? And why is it so elusive (if indeed it is)?

This is the territory I want to explore in this essay. I want to try to set out a positive definition of integrity; to remind ourselves where it has come from in our western moral tradition; and, in the light of this definition and origin, to consider why it is often hard to find, especially in our current social context – yet also why it is still possible to find it. All, of course, with the caveat that I cannot claim to offer a definitive account of integrity, nor that I actually possess it myself to any notable degree!

Meanings of Integrity

Rather like trying to define God, integrity often seems easier to define by what it is not. The Nolan committee's current definition of the principle largely adopts this approach. So, for example, integrity is routinely understood as not being hypocritical (that is, not believing one thing and saying or doing another); not being corrupt (that is, not using a privileged position for personal gain); and not being opportunistic (that is, not disregarding principles in pursuit of self-serving goals).

But can we also provide a more positive definition? I certainly want to try. What I will suggest is that there are a number of ingredients of integrity rather than one formal definition – each important, but none adequate on its own. Crucially, they all need to work together. Real integrity, when analysed, will prove to be a compound concept.

The first ingredient is surely sincerity, by which I mean when we act and speak consistently with our true inner thoughts and beliefs, rather than thinking one thing and doing another; the disposition, therefore, in which our public action is always at one with our current private beliefs and values. In public life, this means consistency between inner and outer selves so that we never use our public role as a refuge to evade the demands of our sincere inner beliefs. So, for example, a government minister has integrity in these terms if their actual policy on education matches their internal personal beliefs about it, which they also hold and act on consistently in their role as a parent.

Sincerity in this sense of being consistently true to oneself in any role is widely acknowledged as a core virtue and commonly assumed as a meaning of integrity. Philosopher Bernard Williams suggests that this 'internal truthfulness' is reckoned to be the foundational virtue of our age in his book *Truth and Truthfulness*.[5] Its popularity fits with an age generally sceptical about deferring to external authorities. Trust in external authority appears an abdication of personal responsibility, whereas inner sincerity has become supreme and a key ingredient of integrity, certainly a necessary condition for it.

But is it a sufficient condition? Williams did not think that, and nor do I. The appeal to sincerity alone can create moral unease as well as moral admiration. One obvious example of this from recent public life is to be found in the prelude to the Iraq War. Former Prime Minister Tony Blair's argument for invading Iraq was pre-eminently an appeal to sincerity. When citing external principles and reasons for action, he tended to shift between them rather than derive any decisive authority from them, oscillating between legal reasons (the United Nations' resolutions), moral reasons (stopping Saddam Hussein's cruelty to his own people), and political reasons (how weapons of mass destruction threatened security). But there was no equivocation when he cited his own sincerity. Here he was consistent. This was his main rhetoric. This, it appears, was what counted most for him. What he personally, 'sincerely', believed seemed sufficient.

Yet it was not sufficient. I do not think it is just with the benefit of hindsight that it has felt inadequate. Regardless of whether the action taken by Blair was ultimately right or wrong, regardless of whether he was actually sincere (something requiring a window to his soul, which I do not have), I suggest there is moral unease felt just in this very procedure of allowing personal sincerity absolute authority. For why should being true to 'myself' (i.e. my current state of belief and perception) have such decisive weight? Is not the self too unreliable? How do we know that our self (Tony Blair's self or any self) has been so well formed that it can bear that weight? What after all *is* our 'self'? Is it not a porous thing, subject to other influences, many unconsciously received? So how do we know it is 'our' self at all? How do we know it is reliable? And even if I could isolate that part of myself which *is* just mine, my own inner process of moral reasoning, why should that be absolutely trusted, exempt from relativism and from the simple skewing of self-interest and sin? Granting an absolute casting vote to 'myself', far from a sufficient condition for integrity, actually seems remarkably inadequate.

Absolutising our own selves like this can be thought of as parallel to the current fashion of absolutising our own identity. In medieval logic our identity tended to mean simply that which distinguishes us from someone else, but that is not what we mean by personal identity now. We mean a more fluid, porous, social notion made up of many ingredients, some inherited from genetic and social forces beyond our control. On that definition, to insist that we can *wholly* choose our own identity, which must then be respected uncritically, is an absurdity. Like absolutised sincerity, this absolute claim to our own identity is ultimately narcissistic. It is also nonsense. As one exasperated philosopher says, identitarianism is just a 'conceptual narcotic': seductive in the way it gives a temporary boost to self-esteem, but false in what it claims.[6] It may satisfy our inner Walter Mitty, but it cannot be true and it is hardly a marker of integrity. Respecting self-identification (or sincerity) is indeed a moral requirement – but absolutising it is not. It is merely a moral cloak for self-idolatry. Integrity clearly needs something else beyond sincerity and our own self-perceptions.

So this leads to a second ingredient: upholding principles. Principles are at best the accumulated wisdom of others and of society, tried and tested over time. They represent a more external source of authority that is less bound to our selves. And this too is surely another obvious and important element of integrity, not least in public life. Adhering to principles is, after all, the positive opposite of general self-centredness; the opposite of the opportunism that overrides public interest for short-term personal gain; the obverse of the cynicism that corrodes public life. It is also the positive engine of trust that cements public life. Having consistent principles generates trust because it reassures others about not just our present actions but future actions too.

The power of principles in practice has ebbed and flowed. Kenneth Clarke's autobiography illustrates some of the shifts of recent times in UK politics.[7] In the so-called conviction politics of the 1980s, both sides of the political divide often appealed, at least in their rhetoric, to principles as a natural currency of political discourse. This contrasts with the discourse of the late 1990s onwards, when policy was apparently shaped more by short-term popularity, public opinion, and self-interest. But although the power of principles in practice has varied, their *value* is rarely disputed. The principled person is almost always regarded highly.

Even so, are principles actually sufficient for real integrity, any more than sincerity? Again I have to say they are not. For a start, there is the prior question of which principles we accept or choose. Self-evidently, not all principles are good! But more radically, are there not also intrinsic limits even to good principles?

Sophocles' celebrated play *Antigone* long ago famously made the case against principles being all-sufficient or absolute.[8] Its basic plot describes a city-state's ruler, Creon, attempting to live by principles. He decrees that any citizen fighting for the enemy who dies must not be buried but left to rot, precisely *as* an important principle of civic honour. And as a man of principle, Creon does not falter. He does not waive this rule even when his own family member (a nephew) is found in this situation. He leaves him to rot. However Antigone, the victim's sister, buries him out of love for her dead brother. But Creon remains resolute and punishes her too by walling her into a cave. He finally relents, but by this time she has committed suicide, so it is too late (a typically cheerful Greek tragedy!).

This is a searching and searing plot for the status of principles. If we define integrity as consistently keeping principles, then we ought to admire Creon. He sticks to his principles, uncorrupted by appeals to make exceptions for his family. Antigone, by contrast, does not. She appears to be without integrity in those terms. She apparently makes no protest about the principle when ordinary citizens were left to rot – only for her own brother. And there is no more integrity in that (in terms of principled action) than objecting to the flogging of a fellow Briton for a cultural crime in, say, Saudi Arabia, but failing to object on behalf of Saudi citizens. Yet admiration for Creon's principled consistency over Antigone's approach is not where the moral logic of the plot points. The play's prophet describes Creon's behaviour not as moral heroism but only as 'stubbornness and stupidity'. The drama seals this verdict when Creon's wife too finally commits suicide, to show even more decisively how blind consistency in one's principles actually leads only to multiple disasters. Nor can we dismiss this moral dilemma of the plot simply as the wrong choice of principle (i.e. a particular and bizarre principle of civic honour). If we try to read the play like this, as merely a critique of the kind of principles Creon maintained (with Antigone now seen as a principled person after all, on the basis she at least adhered to a *good* principle of family loyalty), the drama will subvert this by showing how her actions too will lead to the serial suicides.

In short, this is a play about the ambivalence of principles *per se*. It presents a complex moral universe where personal and civic obligations and principles are in irrevocable conflict and cannot be absolutised without tragedy. In such a world it is precisely by reducing integrity and virtue to simply a code of principles that both Creon and Antigone fail. Only a play? Yes – but like all good plays a window onto real life, and one from which philosophers and public servants from Hegel to the present have found wisdom.[9] It is a stark warning. Consistent principles may be vital and admirable at times. Flip-flopping through life without principles just according to self-interest may well lack integrity. Yet there is always danger in holding fast to principles when they solidify into rigid inflexibility. In this complex world there will be conflicting principles and loyalties that rigidity cannot resolve without doing damage. *Why* the world is inevitably like this (i.e. generating conflicting values and loyalties) is the subject of another essay.[10] The point I am making now is simply that in such a world as this, absolute consistency to principles is just not going to work morally. Absolute consistency on its own is going to be indistinguishable from the terrifying consistency of a single-minded fanatic or terrorist.

So it seems we shall need yet another ingredient, another perspective on integrity. We need a way to live truthfully with irreconcilable conflicting principles. And I shall call this way 'moral irony'. Like sincerity and being principled, it is primarily a disposition of behaviour, and this too may be illustrated to begin with by a drama – in this instance a real life drama, albeit a fictionalised view of it.

The example here lies in the life of the twentieth-century composer Dmitry Shostakovich, someone who clearly had to operate in a world of conflicting interest. His world was the era of the Soviet Union, and the conflict for him was generated by the State's call on artists to be public servants. In this context the dilemma was how he could make music with integrity. The State wanted music to be composed and performed to express its values with predominantly triumphant, heroic, optimistic tones. Yet music must be an expression of free creativity, not captive to any political ideology. It presented Shostakovich with a dilemma where the stakes could not be higher. It was not just the integrity of music at risk. His own life and his family members' lives were also at stake.

The fictionalised account of Shostakovich's dilemma is offered tellingly by Julian Barnes in his novel *The Noise of Time*.[11] What he portrays is the attempt at a resolution through a certain kind of compromise. At one level Shostakovich's music did seem to comply with the State. But in fact much of it was coded. Rather like the visions of the Book of Revelation in the New Testament, which were coded expressions of resistance for early Christians facing the persecutions of Nero, Shostakovich's music was an oblique resistance. It included some conventional tropes for the State to use, but for those with ears to hear it also conveyed genuine, potentially subversive creative freedom. In other words, Shostakovich's actions tried at least to hold together conflicting principles, each of which had some value. His music was an act to safeguard his family's lives, his own life as a composer, and to fulfil a measure of public service; but it was also an act to uphold the principle of free, subversive artistic expression. Shostakovich offered in his music a deliberately oblique expression in order to combine both obligations.

Was this integrity, we might ask? Or was this obliqueness just fudge and a failure of nerve? I cannot judge for him in his particular circumstances. Nor am I holding up Shostakovich as a model of integrity just by virtue of this particular action. But I am suggesting that the *kind* of thing he was trying to do offers a good illustration of what can be integrity. *Prima facie* it might seem the opposite. After all, this sort of oblique approach appears to open up a gap between what we believe and what we actually express. But in fact, in this context, the gap itself expresses a truth: namely, that in situations of complex conflicting principles, truth cannot always be served by adherence to just one principle. Where two or more principles both matter, closing that gap by opting for just one might seem morally clearer but is in fact less truthful to the whole situation. So the simple choice of one overriding principle would actually have less integrity than the oblique approach. I call this obliqueness 'moral irony' as a reference to the way irony is employed in literary terms. The use of gaps and obliqueness in language (or even silence, as Jesus sometimes showed) is an acknowledged means of expressing complex moral realities more truthfully than literal straightforward expression can do.

I believe this kind of integrity is actually being routinely lived out in public life: both by politicians and by civil servants, perhaps especially by the latter. Civil servants do not have to operate in a Soviet-style context, but they do still have to deal with conflicting loyalties and principles, not least in this Brexit era. It is intrinsic to their role. Faced with implementing any policies of which they disapprove, there will inevitably be a conflict between loyalty to conscience and loyalty to the overall democratic principles of government from which a particular policy has emerged. My sense is that it is precisely an attempt to honour both principles that has often led civil servants to an oblique approach. That is, they refuse to short-cut the dilemma either by absolutising the principle of being true to oneself, or by mindlessly absolutising the principle of democratic governance. The preferred approach is often more oblique – illustrated by attempts to mitigate a particular policy *within* the terms of the overall system of governance and procedure; by constructive, not destructive, protests; by drafting other proposals to ameliorate the effects of the problematic policy; in short, by the sort of nudges commended by the Government's own 'nudge' unit, the Behavioural Insights Team. They are all oblique approaches, but surely as such are precisely an attempt at integrity, an authentic part of its meaning.

It is only a part, of course. I suspect we all recognise that there will also be extreme circumstances when obliqueness just will not do, and when one principle must override others, even if it leads to extreme options, such as resignation. Integrity means making that judgement too. In such circumstances perhaps Dietrich Bonhoeffer – the German Lutheran pastor commemorated on Westminster Abbey's west front – is a better model than Shostakovich. When his sense of moral duty to resist Hitler conflicted with his principle of pacifism, he could not find a way of honouring both. So he ended up joining the Resistance and plotting to kill Hitler, demonstrating his integrity in his willingness to sacrifice one principle for another rather than trying to hold them both together in some way.

But extreme circumstances are rare. And even then, the attempt to honour conflicting principles may still play some part in guiding future action, even if it could not succeed in the extreme situation. Bonhoeffer himself found that the principle of pacifism he had to sacrifice still exerted pressure on him later, after his fateful decision was made (something I will return to). So in that sense what is represented by Shostakovich's music does always constitute part of integrity. Trying to hold together conflicting principles, rather than too easily abandoning one just for the sake of some spurious moral clarity, will always matter. It is a kind of integrity regularly assayed in much public life: often misunderstood as lack of integrity, but actually genuine, costly, and admirable.

All of which leads therefore to an overall definition. Integrity, I suggest, may be best understood simply as holding these three endeavours together. It is partly sincerity, being truthful to our inner selves; it is partly drawing on well-tried external principles; and it is partly being willing and able to see the complexity of some situations and act obliquely. Most crucially, the person of integrity is one in whom, consciously or unconsciously, *all* of these ingredients are working together. They are someone who does not suppress any one of these ingredients just for peace of mind, personal comfort, or a quick decision, but who thinks and acts holistically with all these ingredients. In this respect they are a whole person. The Latin origin of the word suggests as much: *integer* means something whole, whose parts are always held together.

What is also implied by this attempt at wholeness is necessarily a dynamic *process*, and not necessarily a static completed whole. After all, if integrity is a continual moral conversation between these ingredients then, as with all such conversations, it will always be a work in progress rather than a perfect possession or settled achievement; a process in which change is likely to play a part, since if we never change our mind it is unlikely we are really engaging in that conversation. This in turn means that honesty and humility will also be key ingredients. To be a person of integrity will always require being honest with ourselves, which enables us to hear what all of these ingredients say to us rather than suppressing any one element for the sake of an easy outcome. It will also require the honesty to hear and truthfully admit any residue of dissatisfaction we may still feel even after listening carefully, so that we are always able to think and say, 'I still may have got it wrong'. That, too, will be part of this integrity.

This sort of honesty is clearly conveyed in Barnes's picture of Shostakovich. He portrays a person who genuinely attempted integrity but still admitted he was dissatisfied. He still had the 'ache to say things straightforwardly'.[12] Bonhoeffer also remained dissatisfied, even after taking a very different approach. Having abandoned ambiguity and having allowed one principle to overrule – for the sake of integrity in extreme circumstances – he then wrote from his prison cell about his unfulfilled aspirations. He still longed for a place where principles did not have to compete at all.[13] These honest dissatisfactions are, I believe, also part of integrity, not a sign of its absence; they are a sign of conscience still alive and active within this complex moral world.

What, then, is integrity? It is honest, open conversation with our inner selves, with others, with external principles, and with reality – holding them all together. And it is always *acting* on this basis, so that we are, in Václav Havel's celebrated phrase, actually '*living* in this truth', not just trying to know it.[14]

Origins of Integrity

As for where it comes from, I think this definition of integrity makes it abundantly clear. It is self-evidently a child of central western moral traditions. It lies squarely in the humanist tradition of both our Cartesian roots and our communitarian instincts; two strands that together have long told us that we are at our best precisely when we act in harmony both with our own inner self and with wider social principles and social relationships. It also fits with more recent western liberal pluralism, with its insistence that moral and social truth lie precisely in the interplay of many principles and values and sources of truth, not in the absolutising of any one ideology or any one principle.

I also believe it relates specifically to Christian tradition – unsurprisingly, since so much western moral thinking has been shaped by a Christian heritage. The sense that the self to which we must be true cannot be absolutised fits like a glove with Christian understandings of what being made as creatures in the image of God means: we are not sealed-off self-sufficient things but intrinsically relational, made out of social relations, like the Trinitarian God. The sense that the principles to which we must be true should also not be absolutised is specifically Christian in the way it echoes both Christ's and St Paul's view of the law. The sense that integrity requires unity between private and public self, between word and action, is Christian because it is rooted in the meaning of incarnation itself, the pre-eminent site where God's own thoughts and words (God's *logos*) have unity with God's own action in a real and complex world. The unity of a person with their role is Christian because it is embedded in the doctrine of Trinity, where God's personhood is conceived as three integrated roles: an understanding of personhood that replaced antiquity's impoverished view that personhood was just a mask we put on and discard when in different roles.

Why So Hard?

But now to the final question. If this is what integrity is, and this is where it comes from, can this shed light on why it also seems so scarce, so hard to achieve, and all too often only a mirage? I think it can. First, simply because trying to be true and honest to *all* these – true to ourselves, to wider principles, and to the full complexity of reality – is always going to be intrinsically hard. It will be much harder than just putting on whatever mask suits us or following whatever principle is in fashion. It will take moral courage, in almost any context. Secondly, by analysing its individual ingredients, this account of integrity has also uncovered dispositions that are particularly difficult and unfashionable, specifically in our current context. Using just the totemic and generic word 'integrity' tends to conceal this. But analysing its ingredients uncovers it.

For example, the notion that integrity means consistency and integration between our private and public selves, whatever role we are in, is at odds with a good deal of prevailing mores, particularly in the workplace. Professionalisation has recently tried to *separate* a person from the role, private from public, elevating the role to its own validity with its separate world of values that are not integrated with the rest of who we are. It is a mask we have to put on with its own value system, one that often includes a measure of ruthlessness and a good deal of economy with the truth. It is part of an instrumentalised work culture where our role at work is deliberately extracted from our private self to achieve efficiency in the corporate aim. A report by the think-tank Demos entitled *Entrepreneurship and the Wired Life* has highlighted how pervasively this has occurred.[15] It is one of the outcomes of our general late-modern social fragmentation, where we have become used to inhabiting different narratives with different values – unlike past social worlds, whether of Aristotle, Christendom, or Jane Austen, where there was little or no notion of having different moral values for different roles. There are signs that this social tide is now turning back to a more integrated view of our selves at work. But we are not there yet. And it is why integrity is hard.

Another unfashionable ingredient uncovered is simply integrity's requirement to open up oneself to wider principles. This is hard because that same wider social fragmentation has meant we do not really have many common trusted principles anyway – so of course it is easier for us to take refuge instead either in just the values of a superficial role or in some inner temple of our own identity sealed off from external values, the opposite of integrity. Again, this shows why integrity on this definition is bound to be hard.

But Still Possible!

So we have to accept it will not be easy. And why not? Why should it be easy? Moral and spiritual traditions from Aristotle to Augustine, secular and religious, have rarely offered virtue on a plate: it has to be learned. But that is not where I want to leave this discussion, just with a sense of its difficulty. As I have made clear, I believe a good deal of oblique behaviour in our public life, easily dismissed as lacking integrity, does actually display it. It is at least an honest attempt, a work in progress. So this much is clearly possible.

I want to note this too. When analysed, integrity may appear hard because it is complex. But when we actually meet someone of integrity, does not this quality appear in them not so much as a complex conversation or calculation, but as something more instinctive? And instinctive dispositions can arise in any of us. They are not so rare or so difficult, particularly if we are well formed; that is, if we are formed in the practices of a moral or spiritual tradition that holds together all these ingredients for us – traditions like our best liberal humanist traditions and our Judaeo-Christian traditions among others, traditions whose stories, beliefs, and practices themselves combine self-knowledge, sound principles, and deep honesty to show us what it is like to be a person of integrity, what sort of life emerges from integrity, a life that then becomes natural for us if we are immersed in these traditions. If, for example, we are formed in a tradition in which we keep hearing prophetic words like 'What does the Lord require of you but to do justly, love mercy and walk humbly with your God' (surely one of the best single synopses of a life of integrity), we shall find ourselves instinctively formed by that vision. In short, if we allow ourselves to be formed by these traditions, integrity *can* be formed 'naturally' in us.

There is a further dimension to this. These traditions also offer resources to sustain us when we fail. This too encourages us to keep trying. Christian faith certainly did this for Bonhoeffer. It was the profound doctrine of grace in his Lutheran tradition that meant that even with his continued sense of dissatisfaction, he still knew he was forgiven, carried, and inspired. That is what kept him still humbly trying. I am not for one moment suggesting here that only those formed specifically in Christian faith can sustain integrity. That is palpably untrue. But I do want to suggest that to belong to some mature spiritual or moral tradition, rather than trying to do it alone, is to have access to a powerful resource.

Integrity is indeed vital. A foundational virtue. A bedrock for trust in both private and public life. And perhaps it is particularly scarce and difficult now. What I hope is that digging deeper has helped to shed light on this. I also hope it has uncovered some grounds for encouragement: the hope that it is not just a mirage; the sense that some nuanced practices may still be part of an attempt at integrity; and the reminder that there are great moral and spiritual traditions that will support us in the quest. We are not alone.

Public Service Institutions:
Custodians or Stiflers of Spirit?

Claire Foster-Gilbert

In Peter de Rosa's 1975 book *The Bee and the Rose*, the individual spirit of the worker bees has been suppressed by the utilitarian demand to be productive. But Bobby the bee has struck up an illegal friendship with a rose whose pollen he had been collecting. She challenges his deep-seated institutionalised beliefs.

'Tell me, why do you always travel in a beeline?'

'Because it's the shortest way to go.'

'Why can't you go by the longest way?'

'But that's silly to go by the longest way when there's a shortcut.'

'That's just where you're wrong, Bobby,' Rosa insisted. 'Haven't you ever watched the butterflies? Why can't you be as carefree as they are? Surely you can see the fun they get by travelling backwards and forwards, up and down.'

'What is **fun**?' asked Bobby.

'**Fun** is doing something because you like doing it and for no other reason.'

'Then,' said Bobby, 'how would we gather all the honey in if we stopped for **fun**?'

'Let me ask you a question first, Bobby,' Rosa said. 'Why are you gathering in all that honey?'

'Because the rules say we must.'

'But isn't there a reason for the rules?'

Bobby said, 'There must be a reason but perhaps only the One who made the rules understands it.'

'Not very convincing,' Rosa went on. 'I've been told that when your beehive is full of honey everyone leaves in one great swarm and sets off in search of another hive – all colourless and empty. Where's the sense in that?'

'You are trying to undermine my faith,' said Bobby angrily – except he remembered the doorkeeper's words that if he were pure of heart he would never feel anger or emotion of any sort. Perhaps he was half enjoying Rosa's temptations.[16]

The actual name of Bobby the bee is 15/753, because he was the fifteen thousand, seven hundred, and fifty-third bee to be born in the hive. He was given a quota of flowers to visit each hour, was not thanked for his work, even when he exceeded his quota, and did not expect to be. He was glad simply to be contributing to the good of the hive. He had been warned against all emotions because they interrupted the smooth running of the hive. But feelings stir in him, despite himself, when a fellow bee is injured and pitilessly banished to the outside where he dies. And then everything goes wrong, and right, for 15/753 when he enters a rose to take her pollen and she wants to know why he had not sought her permission first. That had never happened before. They start talking, and Rosa, for that is her name, gives Bobby his. Despite himself, he likes having his own name, and his faith in the hive system is undermined from that point. He fails to achieve his quota, shouts 'Love! Love! Love!' at his trial, and is outlawed. Shortly thereafter the bee and the rose end their lives together, he resting in her dying petals as the summer draws to a close.

The Individual vs. The Collective

The message of Peter de Rosa's book is that institutions destroy people's individual spirit. If it were not for institutions, people would be free to express themselves fully in their own unique way. However bright and enthusiastic you might be upon arrival in an institution to work, the institution can bear down upon you, stifling your spirit and changing your character. When a new dinner lady first appeared at my primary school, she was lovely to us, a warm maternal presence in the dining room when we came for our lunch. Within a year, however, she had become shrill, ferocious, and unforgiving. I wondered what we had done to her. Many years later, at another institution where I was working, I observed a steward change over time from likeable to abrupt and forbidding. The ethos of the department he was in had changed him. And I heard the frustration of a young campaigner who first interacted with an MP when he was newly elected. He was friendly, slightly nervous, helpful, and accommodating. Eighteen months later he had switched to transmit only, did not listen to her, and was in a tearing hurry. The system had changed him.

In the Civil Service, exciting, lively, new, and internally incoherent political ideas and ideals, presented by the minister to be made to work and of which civil servants will experience plenty in their professional lifetime, will be swallowed into the internal sausage machine of the department and regurgitated as coherent, well-crafted policies whose inconsistencies have been smoothed away, but which no longer reflect the inspiration and integrity of the minister. And then the smooth logic of the policies, however perfectly they work on paper, means that they turn out to be more inhumane than anyone intended when they are put into practice, when the frontline staff have to implement them, when, as it were, they come back to messy life as they are applied to people whose complex circumstances confound neat solutions to housing, education, law enforcement, or borders defining identity. Like the administrations that drew straight lines across British Empire territories and named them borders, regardless of tribe or landscape, the neat policies of rational intellect can betray an expensive lack of emotional understanding and the idiosyncrasies of local knowledge. In the end, a policy is about a person, as W. H. Auden writes in his poem 'Refugee Blues': 'He was talking of you and me, my dear, he was talking of you and me.'[17]

This sacrifice of the individual to the collective does not happen all the time, and civil servants now are only too well aware of the challenges of implementation and delivery. But it does happen, usually in a bid to keep the minister happy and the elected government of the day apparently on track. And there is a powerful *moral* force in the suppression of individual inspiration at the point of turning idea into policy. It is a utilitarian moral force: the greatest good for the greatest number, which inevitably denies the human face of the inspiration. The policy must be fair, rational, and achievable, and therefore countable: it must apply equally, and it must be possible to show that it does. The benefit-cost ratio that governs policy development in some government departments is an efficient and *prima facie* fair way of coming to conclusions about what the policy should be, but it means that everything that needs to be taken into account in the policy has to be made countable, capable of being turned into a number. As more seemingly incommensurable things are included in the benefit-cost calculation, so the task becomes more challenging: how, for example, do you calculate and compare the relative cost of biodiversity loss in building new transport infrastructure, or calculate the benefit of travel that is adapted to older people, not just the economically productive and physically fit? Every person and every place is irreducibly different, and no one's needs are precisely the same as anyone else's. Policies have to serve real people and places, and how can they ever do that if they also have to be nationwide, equally applicable, and reportable in the form of transparent statistics? People are, in the end (thank heavens) incalculable, incomputable.

Values are also incomputable, and trying to turn them into measurable matrices undoes them. I watched one such unravelling happen in the 1990s, when I was involved with the Department of Health in creating a rational system of research ethics committees in Health Authorities, as we called them then. My inspired (as I believed) approach to making a moral judgement about the ethics of medical research involving human subjects was turned into a deadening system of bureaucratic requirements that switched off the researcher's moral sense, as they had to hand the moral decision-making over to the ethics committees, and switched it off in the ethics committees because each had to demonstrate it was making decisions consistently with the other, and how do you do that except with a matrix? The act of trying to ensure consistency and fairness killed the spirit of moral decision-making, as we created a system of ethics committees that avoided postcode lotteries. The process became a tick-box exercise, precisely not what the original conception envisaged. But if we had not had ethics committees and some attempt at consistency, would research subjects, vulnerable patients many of them, be adequately protected? Could we allow researchers to make up their own moral minds? The tension that gives rise to these questions sits at the heart of all institutionalising processes.

The Civil Service institutionalises par excellence, but every public service institution does so too, in its own way. Politicians entering Parliament for the first time fired up with the wish to make a difference may soon find their verve killed. Procedure deadens. Backbenchers learn they have to choose their fights carefully and find causes to join that may not seem authentic to them. Secretaries of State have to win the favour of the Prime Minister and the Treasury if they are to have any hope of their proposed measures becoming reality. Everything is turned, in the institutionalising of politics, into a campaign. If you are part of the Opposition, your campaigns can be forceful and idealistic. If you are part of the Government, you find that the vast majority of your time is swallowed up by un-ignorable pressures that prevent you from making the difference you wanted, of which Brexit has been the latest and greediest example. Even if you do have the chance to introduce measures of your own choosing, what really seems to ensure their successful implementation is not their merit or the knowledge and understanding in you from which they sprang, but how they look to the public, whether they will win votes for your party or lose them for the other party, and, increasingly importantly, whether they can be translated into a simple, binary message. There is no subtlety in this institutionalising of the wish to make a difference. No wonder politicians can look and sound inauthentic.

As President of the Royal Academy, Sir Christopher Le Brun has spoken eloquently about the very great challenge of leading an institution that holds within itself those people who, and that art which, *must* seek to break the bounds of any framework, any institution. Why have an institution for art at all? Will it not simply kill the very inspiration that art depends upon? The Royal Society has a similar challenge – its very existence asserts an interpretation of what science is and who is a scientist, when science, which simply means knowledge, must not be bound by an idea that we already know what knowledge is. Our knowledge can only ever be working hypotheses. So the institution has to define knowledge, and how do you define what must be always free? Westminster Abbey and the religion it embodies has the hardest job of all, one might argue, for it has to institutionalise God, and *of course* if it is institutionalised, it cannot be God.

For any one or more of the reasons articulated above, institutions are, perhaps rightly, regarded with enormous suspicion. One commentator said they were like 'beached whales', stranded in a society that values individual expression and self-chosen identities, and nothing that binds them. The energetic explosion of small businesses and the inexorable rise of the gig economy are symptomatic of this issue. We increasingly proclaim our individual identities, like Rosa, knowing that love must be expressed, and we want to set Bobby free from the utilitarian constraints of a system that does not even recognise him enough to give him a name. We join causes, not organisations, and we let the unity that the cause had us feel with our fellow humans melt away when the cause is no longer being fought. Our loyalty, such as it is, is to the cause, not the structure that might be created to make it possible to fight together for that cause. We will not be bound – or taught – by the past, held in institutional memories. We are mobile beings, connected by our phones not by place. We have never been so free to choose the company we keep. We are the precariat.

Our individualism is characteristic of the age. It is a microcosm of the United Kingdom trying to leave Europe and of Scotland teetering on the brink of leaving the United Kingdom and Wales' own significant movement for independence, themselves characteristic of what has been called the geo-political equivalent of climate change: all around the world countries break away from older blocs where there was some loyalty to the bloc itself, and instead form ad hoc, bilateral partnerships. While apparently more functional in the short term, the fluidity of the configurations and their distinctly utilitarian and self-interested natures mean a global precariat is forming.

What *is* this individual spirit we are so keen to assert, though? Where do we find it when we are bound to nothing? With no supporting structures and no guidance from the past, we flounder in a sea of free choices. Meanwhile, nimble and unprincipled adversaries take advantage of global and local instability and our unyoked, tender young become pathologically anxious.

We have little protection against what Peter Oborne in 2007 presciently called 'manipulative populism'.[18] We demonstrate a worrying desire to find 'masters' to follow, in the form of individuals beloved by the traditional media (headline-creating politicians) and social media (picturesque Instagram influencers). How are we to know whether the charisma and charm of the leaders we venerate mask foolishness or wisdom? However much we value our individuality, we still long to belong to one another. In the absence of stabilising institutions, we are prone to latch onto attractive characters and shallow populist ideological causes, shouting all the louder for them because deep in our hearts we *know* the causes are more complex than our chosen leaders are telling us. Their whole truth will never fit on our placards and in our social media posts.

Meanwhile the forces that dominate our century are all irreducibly communal and pressing: the ecological crisis, migration, technology, security, finance... They can only be addressed by institutions because they require comprehensively thought-through, organised, sustainable, very long-term responses, and no individual can do this for us.

The Importance of Institutions

Institutions are custodians of value in ways individuals can never be, and we cannot do without them. The United Nations has worked for global peace and has partly succeeded for seventy years. The European Union has worked for peace in Europe, and mostly succeeded, for forty years. For over 800 years the UK Houses of Parliament have fallibly but intentionally shaped and protected democracy, ensuring the people do not endure a tyranny. For 150 years the Civil Service has operated, fallibly but intentionally, as a meritocracy, exercising political impartiality, buffering the volatile political world against the inevitable corrosive force of ambition in those who must seek election. For a thousand years the judiciary has evolved into robust independence. For a thousand years universities have nurtured intellectual pioneers. For nearly 400 years the Royal Society has sought to champion the honest and independent search for evidence and supported those whose high calling that is. The Royal Academy has worked for over 150 years to help art retain a profile in the national consciousness, to teach and encourage new artists, to recognise great artists, to ensure that art of all kinds is *seen*. Since humans started writing about those in power, the press has fought to defend its freedom to tell the truth. And without all-too-fallible religion, we would not have rituals that hold people together in times of mourning and celebration, nor would we have ancient wisdom to help recalibrate human virtue, nor the exquisite decoration of the Aziziye Mosque or the beautiful carving of the Hindu Neasden Temple to evoke wonder. For a thousand years in Westminster Abbey – and in so many other holy places – there has been listening beyond the known horizon, whose atmosphere welcomes and changes us still, despite our precarious selves.

Within the institutions that defend the rule of law and peace on our streets, individual endeavours, our burgeoning small businesses, and the gig economy itself have the chance to flourish. Otherwise what recourse do they have to put right unpaid bills, heinous working conditions, or ecologically devastating procurement patterns? Even acts of civil disobedience or marches against unjust practices need clear streets, the protection (not kettling) of the police, and a place like the Houses of Parliament to stand outside and shout at.

Precisely because institutions, despite their failings, are not 'all about me', they are our protection against attractive and powerful individuals and the temptation to ditch important but difficult values like truth and integrity. Without these institutional protections our deepest, most treasured values, such as truth, love, beauty, and goodness, will, to use Marilynne Robinson's unforgettable phrase, '[dissolve in the] acid bath of idle cynicism'.[19] Where else do we turn, when we have forgotten what truth looks like, other than to ancient institutions that were created to be its guardian? It is great institutions like the UN (at a global level) and stable public service institutions (at a national and local level) that have guarded the values that should guide us when we have forgotten what we really value, as we jettison vital moral principles like peace, liberty, justice, truth, beauty, and integrity if they are obstacles to our cause.

A Means of Rediscovering Integrity

It is a conundrum. Institutions threaten both the inspiration and the idiocy of individuals. So what makes institutions effective? What ensures their resilience when individuals are weak from laziness or self-questioning, while at the same time preventing them from stifling individual spirit?

I believe that the answer lies in rediscovering integrity. Institutions are animated by people; people are animated by the spirit within them; integrity holds these together by allowing the spirit of people to infuse the institution. Integrity means we are already part of the whole, but not as mere numbers in a big game only the gods (or the so-called elite) are playing, but as active, contributing, intelligent parts, like the organisms in an ecosystem, not the cogs in a machine. It is the life force within organisms that creates the integrity of the ecosystem, animating evolution. And public service institutions can be like this too: we can think not of the machinery of government but the ecology of government, so that the life force of the individuals is not crushed by institutions but is recognised as the very spirit that animates them.

Understanding institutions as integrated ecologies, we can see how the people who make up an institution are both the recipients of the spirit of previous generations but also add to it. When I sat in the library of Balliol College, Oxford for the first time, a fresher still only half-believing I occupied the seat by right, I felt that my intelligence was growing, as though the studies of the thousands of students seeking knowledge of earlier years had seeped into the stone, their intelligent questioning staying behind long after the students had graduated and gone, making itself available to all porous newcomers. I simply *felt* more intelligent, having felt like an impostor. And then I began to study, adding my spirit, however feeble, to the spirit of the place.

Something similar happens when you walk into a church that has been prayed in for centuries. The atmosphere whispers, a spirit rolls off the carved stone and polished wood, permeates the air you breathe. The prayers of thousands of pilgrims seeking the ineffable remain in the place where they were made long after the people themselves have passed on, and you *feel* quieter, more reflective. Then, if you let them, your heartfelt deeper yearnings emerge, and these enhance the spirit of the place.

And so it is with the experience of sitting in the House of Commons or House of Lords chamber, where on that site (more or less) people have argued legislation into being for hundreds of years. I volunteered to be a dummy MP when the clerks were testing their induction programme in 2015, because Westminster Abbey Institute exists to serve all public servants, including MPs, and I wanted to know how they felt, these raw recruits to a venerable system. I was channelling a 'new MP' attitude while 200 or so of us passed between the forbidding and welcoming statues of Winston Churchill and Lloyd George into the chamber, and sat on the green benches, as of right, for the first time. It was everything you might imagine: terrifying, uplifting, humbling. I felt the command of responsibility in the place, calling the spirit of the next generation of politicians to wake up and attend to the good of the nation. Real MPs heard and responded to that command, adding their attention to the spirit of the place.

College, church, chamber, all can summon a greatness of spirit out of the puny-feeling individual who joins them, so that the spirit of the individual and the spirit of the place conjoin. The integrity of an institution is to be found where the endeavour of all those who have passed through leaves its impress, so that as the new soul enters the portals of an institution for the first time, both it and they are enhanced. The spirit of the place is regenerated by new additions and the spirit of the person expands to realise greater potential and fulfilment. It was people who left their spirit in the places of learning, worship, and debate for the student, pilgrim, and MP to breathe in, and it will be they in turn who breathe out a new spirit that carries the integrity of the tradition, imbued with new life.

It was the institutions of government, not individuals, that ensured a degree of stability following the 'leave' result of the Brexit referendum in the summer of 2016. Civil servants, having been paralysed by shock, and in many cases grief, on Friday 24 June 2016, came into work on Monday morning with their sleeves rolled up, following the tradition of making new ideas – whether they agree with them or not – work as best they can for the country. The institutionalised approach, for all its drawbacks, was what sustained them; and their readiness to adhere to the Civil Service value of political impartiality in turn strengthened an institution that is vital to our mature democracy. During those exciting early summer months, as politicians ran around like ants in a disturbed nest, breaking and re-forming allegiances and looking for new nests and niches to operate from, as journalists breathlessly told the news and hazarded guesses at political developments (not quickly enough to be ahead of developments that were, in fact, more interesting than anyone could make up), as the public looked at its neighbour and wondered who on earth they were after all, the civil servants worked steadily on. They continue to do so. The stable service that the Civil Service has shown in response to the Brexit referendum is outstanding and will leave its spirit in the institution for those who join in the years to come.

That determined adherence to the Northcote-Trevelyan spirit of the Civil Service in July and August 2016 carried the other public service institutions for a time, and by the end of the summer there was a new government in place and the politicians at least knew where their seats were in the Chamber again, more or less. Soon after the Judiciary played its constitutional role, establishing that judges could only administer law made in Parliament and therefore Parliament, not a referendum, had to change the law in relation to the EU. In turn this had an animating effect on Parliament as its Members recollected their role and responsibility. MPs and then Peers wrestled with their consciences, their allegiances, the loyalties they owed, the people they serve, in order to debate and vote. This was as it should be: the people elected and appointed to govern should be wrestling with the decision because it *is* difficult, and there is no easy or right answer. So also should the press be criticising everything. We may wince at their words and be furious with their headlines, but at least they are articulated without fear of being silenced or persecuted.

Individual Integrity Creates Institutional Integrity

Institutions are maintained by the active and loyal agency of people working with them. Vernon White has coined the phrase 'creative loyalty'[20] to articulate the nature of this lively, critical engagement. We recall the spirit – the *raison d'être* and values – of our institutions and rekindle it to ensure they continue to serve their purpose, not blindly or unthinkingly, but intelligently and creatively. People within Parliament must assert their right and play their part in holding the Government to account. Civil servants within the Executive must assert their right and play their part in telling ministers how it is – not how they, particularly now, desperately want it to be. Judges within the Judiciary must continue to judge without fear or favour and assert the critical importance of equal access to justice. Academics within universities must defend the value of learning in the face of populist dismissals of expertise and the pressure to commodify students. National leaders must defend their countries and resist nationalist self-interest. Member states must animate the UN to continue to defend the values upon which the whole of humanity and the planet itself depend. And so on. We receive the spirit of an institution, and we carry the responsibility to keep that spirit alive by the animating service of our own spirit of integrity, perhaps never more so than now.

To press the point about agency home: everyone in an institution receives the legacy of integrity and shares the responsibility to pass it on enhanced in value. Not just the leader. We are far too susceptible, at present, to the beguiling charisma of leaders who inspire their followers, persuading, cajoling, or dictating them into sharing their vision, a vision that is unlikely to survive when the leader is found wanting and moves on, as they inevitably will, and people are exposed to another vision. The leader themself is vulnerable to over-identification with a role and an institution, such that their own sense of who they are does not survive their departure either. The vision of an institution should be found, not made, in those who work there, and it should also be constantly re-invigorated by them. They 'create value' as Andrew Kakabadse puts it, by means of properly delegated and supported discretionary judgement.[21] The leader joins a tradition, adding their own value, shaping the next chapter in the life of the institution, which might of course involve a great deal of change, but never for its own sake. This kind of leadership is like gardening, tending the diverse plants that will flourish in the right conditions and enhance each other by their proximity. It is *not* like oiling the mindless cogs in a heartless machine.

Institutions are full of dangers and disadvantages. We often feel more victim than agent, more like Bobby the bee than Rosa the rose. Proper delegation, which means people know, and *feel*, they have moral responsibility, avoids this. Everyone should have their own measure of discretionary judgement. But just as institutions need to be places where people's feeling of moral responsibility is enhanced, not diminished, so people need to remember the value and importance of institutions. Integrity means both. Out of laziness or inattention we can fail to notice how much of our stability and peaceful living is secured by our institutions, where, as Peter Hennessy puts it in our book *The Moral Heart of Public Service*, 'Votes prevail... Raised voices: yes; raised fists: no. That is why Parliaments exist.'[22] We do not want our institutions to be like beached whales whose value no one remembers to care about. Without active engagement with them, they are threatened.

Bobby the bee did need the hive, and he did need to contribute to the making of sweetness in the form of honey; but he was also a vital a part of a wider stable ecosystem. The hives, our institutions, are formed by those who went before us and we are their beneficiaries. We breathe in the cultural air they made for us. We breathe out, and our breath will change that air. That is a responsibility worth bearing well, one over which to take time and trouble, because there are some values and some protections we cannot afford to lose.

Serving the General Public: Mission Impossible?

Jane Sinclair

In his book *Welcome to Everytown: A Journey into the English Mind*, philosopher and writer Julian Baggini seeks to identify the dominant philosophy of England and whether it is sustainable.[23] In order to research his book, Baggini recognised that he needed to look beyond the facts and figures provided by the ever-increasing number of opinion polls and to engage with the people whose thoughts these polls described. Initially, he needed to identify a place that contained what he describes as 'all types of the English'. The place turned out to be a large section of Rotherham. In 2005 Rotherham had the postcode area with the closest match of household types to the country as a whole. The postcode district of S66 had the most typical mix of wealthy pensioners, struggling families, aspiring singles, and so on, with a 93 per cent match to the national data set. The neighbouring postcode area of S25 was the fourth closest match to the national data set. Baggini had found his Everytown.

In the prologue to his book, Baggini lists some of the values and characteristics he expected to find in Rotherham, making no attempt to mask his prejudices. The list was drawn up before he moved to Rotherham for his research proper.

I thought there would be toleration for difference, but no real love for it, and only as long as it was perceived not to be threatening. There would be provincialism. People's aspirations would be modest, or else for superficial things like fame or wealth. The best life would be comfortable and fun. People would think religion was for weirdos and philosophy for boffins. Anti-intellectualism would be rife. People would have their philosophies of life, which would be simple, but true: be thankful for what you've got, make the most of what you have; time waits for no man. Although in behaviour most people would be sexually liberal, most would still want to be married and think that children deserve two married parents. There would be a thin line between having some youthful fun and being a slag. Homophobia would be normal. Despite the talk of a national culinary renaissance, people would still eat badly and the 'best restaurant around' would be rubbish. People would have several fears which are not just founded in their actual experience. Crime, the youth of today and so forth would worry people, even though S66 is probably a fairly quiet area. There would be cynicism, especially about politicians. They would say the television is full of trash but they'd still watch it all the time. They would have a sense of who they were and what their kind were, and would be keen to differentiate themselves. The much-heralded decline of identity would turn out to be overstated. But overall most people would be pleasant and decent.[24]

Baggini reflects on this list two years later, and after his research is complete:

[T]hree things strike me. The first is how critical and condescending a lot of it sounds. The second is nonetheless how little turned out to be totally wide of the mark.[25]

He makes the point that a caricature of the truth may still be true, but does not necessarily go deep enough. You have a first impression on meeting someone: they are boisterous and extrovert, witty, yet apparently unreflective. But on deeper acquaintance, you may discover an inner sensitivity, a desire to be understood, a longing for personal meaning and purpose. The first impression is still true – but it is not the whole truth.

The third observation that Baggini makes is that his list of characteristics, whilst largely true of the area of Rotherham he engaged with, does not really reveal anything about any 'national philosophy' of Englishness. Rotherham is, finally, Rotherham. It is not Dover, or Glasgow, or Larne, or Llandudno; nor is it the hamlets of Swaledale, Bodmin Moor, or the Lincolnshire Wolds. Rotherham has been through very tough times over the past thirty years. But that said, it is a place of great potential with a gritty, no-nonsense, and proud population, most of whom long for – and work hard to see – the place to be thriving once again. I know the town well and love the people: I was the Vicar of Rotherham for just over four years at the time when Baggini was doing his research. And I have been deeply saddened to follow the appalling stories of abuse that have emerged from Rotherham in the years since I left. Sadly, these stories of abuse appear not to be peculiar to Rotherham; rather, they are an indicator of Rotherham's 'typicality' of English community life.

The 'General Public'

I have cited Baggini at length simply to make the point that describing tightly what might be termed 'the general public' is a minefield, and pretty much doomed to failure from the outset. Ask anyone about the 'general public' and you are likely to receive an answer along the lines of 'the general public are people like me'. But 'me' is not you, or her, or them. Individually, and in all sorts of different groupings and networks and interest groups, everyone resident in the UK forms what might be called 'the general public' – and even then, of course, we must add those who are visiting the UK at any one time, and those who are UK citizens but are abroad for a variety of reasons. (The premise underlying this essay is that the 'general public' is, broadly speaking, all those who are resident in the UK today, of whatever age, nationality, background, political persuasion, or any other category you choose to name. UK residence is my yardstick.)

Civil servants, politicians, and those involved in any sort of public service – voluntary or paid – will recognise the challenges of definition. Not surprisingly, serving the general public takes on many different guises. Take some of our large public institutions: Parliament, the National Health Service, and the Church of England, to name but three. All are charged with serving the general public of the UK or, in the case of the Church of England, the general public of England. How do they set about fulfilling their brief?

The Westminster Parliament is constitutionally at the centre of all national law-making. Its legitimacy as the legislature that can and should create law for the whole general public of the United Kingdom lies in its democratic credentials: all

Members of Parliament are elected by those eligible and registered to vote in the UK. But the role of elected MPs, and alongside it the work of members of the House of Lords, is linked with some considerable subtlety to the role of the head of state – the monarch – and to the UK's independent judiciary. Elected MPs have the responsibility of ensuring that the local concerns of their constituency are adequately represented within the larger national concerns of Parliament as a whole, and that national priorities are properly represented back to their constituencies. Devolved government in Scotland, and to a lesser extent in Wales and Northern Ireland, has sought to give regional responsibility in carefully defined areas of tax and expenditure, and some other policy areas. In other words, it is recognised that a working balance has to be found to enable the national legislature to act for the whole of the UK population in areas of activity where the national interest is at stake – say, in defence policy or international relations – and other areas of concern which might reasonably be dealt with at a more local level – say, in social care provision. And all of this is caught up within long-standing and still evolving British constitutional custom and practice, unwritten and complex as it is.

The National Health Service is similarly challenged: how should it provide fair access to the best quality of health care across the whole of the UK, bearing in mind the limited resources available and the ever-growing expectations of the population? The answer is very much a work in progress, and not an easy work in progress at that. Where should specialist hospitals or clinics be sited? How can we best ensure access to good quality health care for those who do not live in urban areas, and where public transport is difficult? These questions can be multiplied many times over. What is often depicted as an intractable problem for the NHS is in fact a challenge to all of us. Are we prepared to pay for the health service we want? If not, who is to make the decisions about where resources should be focused, and on what grounds are the decisions to be made? What priority should the most vulnerable in society have in calls upon NHS resources? Who *are* the most vulnerable; who should decide who they are; and on what grounds? Should decisions be made nationally, or locally?

The Church of England is the public institution with which I am most familiar. As the Established Church, it has always made itself available to every resident in England. Every inch of the country – barring royal peculiars like Westminster Abbey – falls within a Church of England parish. And every parish resident, no matter what their beliefs or lack of them, has the right to be baptised and to be married in their parish church. Parish clergy have to live in their parish and to serve their parishioners as their parish priest. From Middlesbrough to Huish Episcopi, the Church of England has ordained and lay people on the ground, living and working alongside local residents. The parish clergy can claim with some credibility to know who the general public are in their patch. The downside is that it is notoriously difficult to get the Church of England as a whole to act nationally. The General Synod, the House of Bishops, the Archbishops: all can claim to speak for the Church of England and the public whom it serves, but none necessarily does so in practice, whatever the press may choose to think. What happens in any parish may bear little relationship to what the national Church proclaims as Church of England policy.

There are thousands of other national organisations and networks that serve the general public: major retail chains; large service industries, including banks and building societies; leisure and sports organisations; cultural organisations; and the major voluntary sector organisations, among others. But the difference between most of these organisations and those outlined above is that they are in a position to choose the parts of the public with whom they wish to engage. Those in the business of manufacturing and selling goods will identify their market or markets and ignore others. They are engaged in making a profit for their shareholders. Charities, who are not in the business of making profits, focus their work on the section of the public they wish to serve. But those charities will be equally focused on fundraising from a wider but nonetheless carefully defined tranche of grant-giving organisations, as well as the general public as a whole. In short, to understand what is meant by the 'general public' you need not only to understand the broad concept of 'general public' and its complexities; you need also to understand the standpoint of the person describing the general public that they are serving, describing, or engaging with.

Policymaking and Public Service Engagement

There are two areas of public service engagement that may help to identify some of the drivers that shape the success, or lack of success, of this public service engagement. I am indebted to Professors Graham Smith and J. A. Chandler, on some of whose work I will draw for this analysis. In his book *Public Policy and Private Interest*, Chandler explores the complexities of public policymaking processes. This is the stuff of everyday life for civil servants and politicians: it is the major means by which service of the general public is experienced day by day. As Chandler comments, 'The importance of any public policy is … for most citizens not primarily how it is made but the consequences of its content to them as individuals'.[26] Hence the instant analysis of any budget tax proposal by financial experts in terms of the cost-benefit consequences it will have for the individual and their family.

Chandler goes on to argue that the content of public policy in the UK is a reflection of a combination of ideological and ethical values and self-interest, a result of compromises made within groups rather than by a single individual. That is only to be expected, given the number of people who must be consulted and convinced of a public policy case in the UK polity for it to be implemented effectively. The result can be that the interests of the general public, or of a section of the general public, sometimes take second place behind the horse-trading of policymakers. Compare the 1980s BBC television series *Yes, Minister* and *Yes, Prime Minister* to the novels *Wolf Hall* and *Bring Up the Bodies*.[27] *Yes, Minister* may be more contemporary and funnier than the fictionalised Machiavellian activities of the Tudor court, but both forms of storytelling speak truthfully of the power play at work in public policymaking.

It was Thomas Hobbes who coined the phrase, 'No arts; no letters; no society; and which is worst of all, continual fear and danger of violent death; and the life of man solitary, poor, nasty, brutish, and short'.[28] Without civilising institutions, chaos will ensue, argues Hobbes. One definition of effective public policy is that it is a means by which the general public is protected from what would otherwise be the chaos of natural

events and the unintended accidents that result from uncoor-
dinated and self-interested human actions.[29] A more positive
approach would be to argue that effective policymaking is a
way of serving the general public by the promotion of goodness: enabling social groups and human society as a whole to
flourish. Termites can make wonderful termite hills because
of their superb biological programming, but as far as we know
they are not aware of goodness as such. Humans are capable of
identifying values that are important to us and then shaping
our behaviour accordingly, individually and as a society. At its
best, public policy can be shaped from cooperation, as well as
from the struggles and compromises between self-conscious
individuals with very different ideas about what is important
to them and to others.

Conversely, when public policy is seen to be hijacked by
a particular interest group, or is seen to be unfair and unjust,
there will almost inevitably be trouble: challenges in the
courts, vilification in the press, at worst riots on the streets.
You have only to recall the disastrous proposals to implement
a Poll Tax in 1989 (Scotland) and 1990 (England and Wales)
and the so-called Bedroom Tax in 2013 to see what can go
wrong when public policy is perceived to be fundamentally
unfair and unjust.

If public policy relates to enabling humans to flourish, it is
important that those who form and implement public policy
have a deep understanding of how we as individuals conduct
our lives, and how we ought to behave as humans. Human
beings are not ultimately statistics, nor constituencies, nor
networks, nor focus groups. Members of the general public
are people who are shaped by their cultures and values, who

have aspirations for themselves and others, who make mistakes and pick themselves up again, who are moral and spiritual beings, and who long for purpose and fulfilment in their lives. The ethical dimensions of how individuals and groups should behave are important to all of us – whether we are conscious of this or not. Public policy needs to be properly informed by these issues and priorities, and not simply devised to suit economic or party political needs and aspirations.

There are naturally differences of opinion between members of the general public about the ethical dimensions of our lives, but this should be the subject of debate and engagement in policymaking. How diverse and inclusive a society do we wish to be? How diverse and inclusive a society *should* we be? What value do we put on the life of a migrant seeking help from the UK? On what ethical grounds should some people in society pay less tax than others? I have barely scratched the surface of the complex issues bound up in the formation and implementation of public policy as a means of serving the general public.

Turning from public policy to public participation in democratic processes may help us to explore these issues in a different context. Professor Graham Smith is best known for his work on public participation in democratic processes. In his seminal book *Democratic Innovations*, Smith explores some alternative forms of democratic engagement as possible means of increasing the participation of a much wider range of citizens in political decision-making.[30] He outlines the evidence of public disillusionment with institutions of advanced industrial democracies. Numbers of those voting in local and general elections indicate a gradual decline, over many years, in electoral turnout. Opinion polls indicate continuing low levels of trust in politicians and political institutions. Although Smith was writing in 2009, the Veracity Index published by Ipsos MORI in 2015 still indicates that government ministers and politicians are the least trusted to tell the truth of all the professions, bumping along at 21 to 22 per cent.[31] Even estate agents come in at 25 per cent, better than politicians. Civil servants achieve a 59 per cent trust rating, and clergy 67 per cent. All of these are outclassed by hairdressers at 69 per cent and, best of all, doctors at 89 per cent.

Writing prior to the significant changes to the membership of the Labour Party during 2016, Smith comments that generally there has been a decline in the membership of traditional mobilising organisations such as political parties and trade unions. The challenges that a sense of disconnection then poses can be severe and self-perpetuating. As Anne Phillips commented as long ago as 1995, 'when policies are worked out *for* rather than *with* a politically excluded constituency, they are unlikely to engage all relevant concerns'.[32] Smith has argued much more recently that perhaps this was reflected in the Brexit vote: 'If the Brexit result tells us anything, it is that large parts of the population feel alienated from the political process. Opening up new forms of political participation to hear the voices of the politically marginalised is thus critical for the wellbeing of our polity.[33]

Smith proposes that a growing disconnection between citizens and decision-makers does not mean that citizens are necessarily less committed to democratic norms and values.[34] He has undertaken two pilots or experiments in democratic innovation that demonstrate this argument. Assembly North (held in Sheffield) and Assembly South (held in Southampton) were two citizens' assemblies held as part of the Democracies Matter project. Taking place in October 2015, the assemblies differed slightly from one another. Assembly North was a classic citizen-only model. Assembly South was mixed, with a proportion of local politicians alongside citizens. Those who took part in these assemblies were asked to reflect on the experience. From their responses, and the very fact that they were prepared to take part in the enterprise at the outset, Smith demonstrates that given the opportunity to participate in significant decision-making, otherwise unengaged UK citizens are perfectly prepared to step up.

Democratic innovations such as those advocated by Smith may prove to be one means of addressing the aspects of the UK's democracy that have been weakened, or are failing, for various reasons: over-complexity of process leading to lack of transparency and popular control; political or other pressures leading to lack of considered judgement; or a public perception that significant decision-making is for a political elite alone, leading to lack of inclusivity.

As with the formation of public policy, the means by which the general public can participate in the democratic process in the UK have ethical implications. Meaningful participation – a sense that it is worth voicing opinions and questions, that as citizens we are interdependent and that our future is bound up with the wellbeing of our neighbours – is key to the maintenance of a healthy democracy. We should not be embarrassed to say that we are all 'our brother's keeper'. This is an ethical imperative. It should mean that we are concerned to ensure that the marginalised and those whose voices are often drowned out in the mêlée of political and cultural celebrity are given a voice and are listened to carefully. It should mean that we celebrate diversity among the general public and seek to recognise it as a strength in public life rather than a threat or a weakness. It should mean that we sometimes question nationally, regionally, and locally whether the majority's wish is necessarily the right wish. How can our democratic processes better inform, reflect, and enable the creation of a good, generous, and caring society; one that seeks to curb our human tendency to cause harm to others, and promotes instead the common good?

Driving Public Policy: Trust, Integrity, and Hope

What is striking about these areas of public policy development and democratic innovation is that their success, or lack of it, appears to be shaped by some basic underlying drivers – drivers that when they are in place help to build the public confidence necessary for the life of society as a whole to flourish. Three significant drivers, among many others, might be identified.

The first of these drivers is *trust*: trust between political decision-makers and the electorate, trust between citizens themselves, trust between those who create public policy and those who must live within its bounds. The existence of trust does not mean that accountability should be treated lightly – we are fallible, and proper accountability is a means of ensuring that mutual trust is well founded and secure. Well-founded trust enables sufficient belief in the democratic process for that process to work well, including all who wish to participate in it, with transparency of process and the resources needed for considered judgement. A sufficient degree of trust may also enable public policy to be developed with proper respect towards those on whom it will impact, and with confidence that any difficulties that are encountered will be voiced, listened to, and dealt with properly and efficiently.

But the trust of the general public in a political or civil service elite cannot be assumed. There is plenty of evidence that a lack of trust leads to an unwillingness to participate, suspicion of the motives and processes used by those in public service, and a tendency to treat lightly those policies that an individual or community finds unwelcome. The undermining of trust in public institutions and in those who work in them can be deeply corrosive. This is why the *Daily Mail*'s November 2016 headline damning High Court judges as 'Enemies of the People' was outrageous.[35] By all means be critical of judicial decisions, but beware the damage caused by undermining public trust in an independent judiciary and thus in the British constitution as a whole.

The second driver underlying the success of public policy and democratic innovation is that of *integrity*. Integrity essentially means 'one-ness', or wholeness. It encompasses such qualities as honesty, transparency, and consistency. To be a person or an institution with integrity means that you will seek to act for the greater good of the whole, and not out of mere self-interest. You will seek to promote the flourishing of the general public. To act with integrity means that you, individually or as an institution, are worthy of the public's trust and respect. You will take a long and wide and carefully considered view before advocating policy. You will actively seek out diverse opinion in order to listen, to test ideas, to seek wisdom and truth beyond your own or beyond that of your peer group. With integrity as your moral compass, you will be prepared to steer the taxing course between the blind application of principle or political dogma and an unprincipled, inconsistent appeal to personal conscience alone. You will seek to avoid the mantra of 'anything goes, as long as most people are happy most of the time'.

The third driver, which is related to trust and integrity, is *hope*. In order to enter into the trustful relationships needed to make a democratic society work, and in order to develop effective public policy, the general public and those who serve it as politicians or civil servants need to believe that the whole project is worth their time and effort: that it is 'hope-ful' work in which they are engaged. There is no point in devising a new policy for tax, or reforming the NHS, or even opening a new church, if it is not intended to bear fruit for the greater good. The hope cannot simply be the wishful thinking of the few. To bear fruit, the hope has to be genuinely held and worked for by those for whose benefit it is given. To ask ourselves, of any public policy under discussion or any change to our democratic process, 'How does this embody real, life-transforming hope for the future?', to ask the public to imagine what that hopeful future might look like – that is to begin to help the public own the purpose and the goal of our life together.

Trust, integrity, and hopefulness are three of many drivers underlying the qualities of public service. Integral to the importance of all three in public life is that these qualities need to be named and shared as public values – unashamedly, and robustly. Would it not be good to move away from public policy as damage limitation, and more towards public policy as promoting all that makes for human flourishing? Would it not be good to have democratic processes of which people are proud and with which they are glad to engage, which are seen to deliver democratic goods for all to enjoy?

The question remains: is the service of the general public a mission impossible? No, it is not an impossible mission – but it is a very demanding one, and it is always going to be a work in progress needing transparency, mutual respect, and truthfulness, with our energies working to build mutual trust and a high degree of personal and public integrity.

We have come a long way from Rotherham in 2007, and the town has been very publicly and painfully humiliated. However, significant progress has been made. Government commissioners have finished their work, and the control of council functions has been handed back to locally elected people. The courage of a whistleblower brought the abuse scandal to public attention, so much so that action had to be taken. The ensuing spotlight brought all sorts of other failings to light in terms of wider local government practice and public policy failure. Heads have rolled, and there has been much soul-searching among Rotherham residents. But there are signs now of the rebuilding of trust, a recognition of the importance of personal and public integrity, and the growth of new hope among the public of Rotherham. What can be true of Rotherham can be true of us all.

Notes

1   The essay in which Kant argued that you should never
    lie, even if it means that another will be harmed, is
    Immanuel Kant, *On a Supposed Right to Tell Lies from
    Benevolent Motives* [1797], (New York, SophiaOmni,
    2012).

2   Julian Baggini, *Welcome to Everytown: A Journey into the
    English Mind* (London, Granta, 2007).

3   Stephen L. Carter, *Integrity* (New York, Harper
    Perennial, 1996).

4   Committee on Standards in Public Life, *The Seven
    Principles of Public Life* (London, CSPL, 1995).

5   Bernard Williams, *Truth and Truthfulness: An Essay in
    Genealogy* (Princeton, NJ, Princeton University Press,
    2002).

6   Jonathan Rée, review of Vincent Descombes, *Puzzling
    Identities* (Cambridge, MA, Harvard University Press,
    2016), *Times Literary Supplement*, 8 June 2016, www.
    the-tls.co.uk/articles/private/vive-la-difference.

7   Kenneth Clarke, *Kind of Blue: A Political Memoir*
    (London, Pan Macmillan, 2017).

8   Sophocles, *Antigone*, ed. and trans. Reginald Gibbons
    and Charles Segal (Oxford, Oxford University Press,
    2007).

9   Rowan Williams, *The Tragic Imagination* (Oxford, Oxford University Press, 2016).

10 See Vernon White, 'Idealism: exploring the implications of our thwarted ideals', in Claire Foster-Gilbert (ed.), *The Moral Heart of Public Service* (London, Jessica Kingsley Publishing, 2017), pp. 125–40.

11 Julian Barnes, *The Noise of Time* (London, Jonathan Cape, 2016).

12 Ibid., p. 86.

13 Dietrich Bonhoeffer, *Letters and Papers from Prison* (London, SCM Press, 1953).

14 Václav Havel, *Living in Truth* (London, Faber and Faber, 1990).

15 Fernando Flores and John Gray, *Entrepreneurship and the Wired Life: Work in the Wake of Careers* (London, Demos, 2000).

16 Peter de Rosa, *The Bee and The Rose* (Niles, IL, Argus Communications, 1975), pp. 46–9.

17 W. H. Auden, 'Refugee Blues', *Collected Shorter Poems 1930–1944* (London, Faber and Faber, 1973), p. 256, l. 18.

18 Peter Oborne, *The Triumph of the Political Class* (London, Simon and Schuster, 2007), p. xvii.

19 Marilynne Robinson, 'Integrity and the Modern Intellectual Tradition', in *What Are We Doing Here?* (New York, NY, Farrar, Straus and Giroux, 2018), pp. 269–70. First articulated in her Charles Gore Lecture delivered for Westminster Abbey Institute on 7 February 2017.

20 Vernon White, 'Stability: Recovering the Lost Icon of Creative Fidelity', in *The Moral Heart of Public Service*, pp. 193–208.

21 Andrew Kakabadse, *The Success Formula: How Smart Leaders Deliver Outstanding Value* (London, Bloomsbury, 2015), pp. 11ff.

22 Peter Hennessy and Claire Foster-Gilbert, 'Reflections: Timeliness and Timelessness', in *The Moral Heart of Public Service*, p. 252.

23 Baggini, *Welcome to Everytown*.

24 Ibid., pp. 6–7.

25 Ibid., p. 7.

26 J. A. Chandler, *Public Policy and Private Interest* (London, Routledge, 2017), p. 1.

27 Anthony Jay and Jonathan Lynn, *Yes, Minister* (BBC, 1980–84) and *Yes, Prime Minister* (BBC, 1986–8). Hilary Mantel, *Wolf Hall* (London, Fourth Estate, 2009) and *Bring Up the Bodies* (London, Fourth Estate, 2015).

28 Thomas Hobbes, *Leviathan* [1651], ed. Richard Tuck (Cambridge, Cambridge University Press, 1996), ch. 13.

29 Chandler, *Public Policy*, p. 3.

30 Graham Smith, *Democratic Innovations: Designing Institutions for Citizen Participation* (Cambridge, Cambridge University Press, 2009).

31 Ipsos MORI, 'Veracity Index – Trust in Professions 2015' Ipsos MORI Social Research Institute report, available at www.ipsos.com/sites/default/files/migrations/en-uk/files/Assets/Docs/Polls/

ipsos-mori-veracity-index-2015-topline.pdf (accessed 12 September 2019).

32 Anne Phillips, *The Politics of Presence* (Oxford, Oxford University Press, 1995), p. 19.

33 Graham Smith and Alex Sakalis, 'The Problem with Politicians and Democracy', interview for the World Forum for Democracy, 2016, available at www.opendemocracy.net/en/problem-with-politicians-and-democracy (accessed 12 September 2019).

34 Smith, *Democratic Innovations*, p. 4.

35 The headline was published on 4 November 2016. See Wikipedia, s.v. 'Enemies of the People (headline)', https://en.wikipedia.org/wiki/Enemies_of_the_People_(headline) (accessed 12 September 2019).

Commons and Lords: A Short Anthropology of Parliament
by Emma Crewe

*The European Identity: Historical and
Cultural Realities We Cannot Deny*
by Stephen Green

*Breaking Point: The UK Referendum
on the EU and its Aftermath*
by Gary Gibbon

Brexit and the British: Who Are We Now?
by Stephen Green

These Islands: A Letter to Britain
by Ali M. Ansari

Lion and Lamb: A Portrait of British Moral Duality
by Mihir Bose

Drawing the Line: The Irish Border in British Politics
by Ivan Gibbons

Not for Patching: A Strategic Welfare Review
by Frank Field and Andrew Forsey

A Love Affair with Europe: The Case for a European Future
by Giles Radice

Fiction, Fact and Future: The Essence of EU Democracy
by James Elles